For Saul, SS
For Anne, SN

First published in Great Britain in 2001 by Zero To Ten Limited
327 High Street, Slough, Berkshire, SL1 1TX

Publisher: Anna McQuinn
Art Director: Tim Foster
Publishing Assistant: Vikram Parashar

Copyright © 2001 Zero to Ten Limited
Text copyright © 2001 Simona Sideri,
Illustrations copyright © 2001 Sheilagh Noble

All rights reserved.

No part of the publication may be reproduced or utilized in any form or by any means, electronic or mechanical, including photocopying, recording or by any information retrieval system, without the prior written permission of the Publishers.

A CIP catalogue record for this book is available from the British Library.

ISBN 1-84089-144-0

Printed in Hong Kong

Let's look at FEET

Written by
Simona Sideri

Illustrated by
Sheilagh Noble

Look, feet are fantastic!

How many toes on each?

An elephant has five toes too.

But elephants' feet are much bigger than ours.

Horses have hard hooves...

Great for galloping!

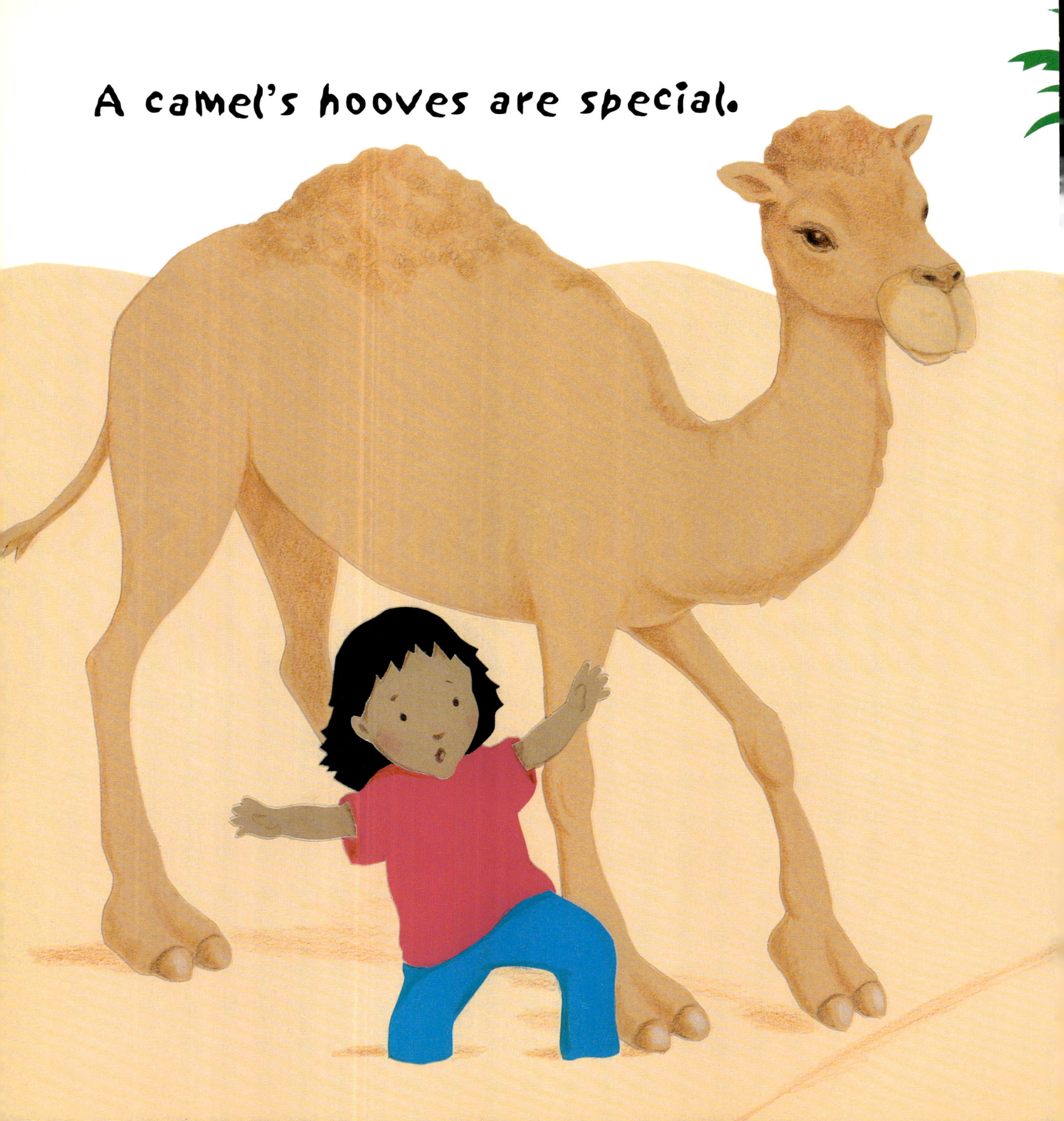
A camel's hooves are special.

They have two toes that spread out flat so the camel doesn't sink in soft sand.

They curl round branches and cling on tightly.

A duck-billed platypus has webbed feet to help it swim swiftly...

and dive deep.

They have sticky pads on their feet.

Feet are **fantastic!**

Some are fast and some are fancy...

But mine are best for me!